D0792234

DREADFUL FATES

Published by arrangement with A & C Black Publishers Ltd.

Text © 2010 Tracey Turner
Illustrations © 2010 Sally Kindberg

Kids Can Press acknowledges the financial support of the Government of Ontario, through the Ontario Media Development Corporation's Ontario Book Initiative; the Ontario Arts Council; the Canada Council for the Arts; and the Government of Canada, through the BPIDP, for our publishing activity.

Published in Canada by
Kids Can Press Ltd.
25 Dockside Drive
Toronto, ON M5A 0B5

Published in the U.S. by
Kids Can Press Ltd.
2250 Military Road
Tonawanda, NY 14150

www.kidscanpress.com

Cover illustration by Maya Gavin

This book is smyth sewn casebound.
Manufactured in Singapore, in 10/2010 by Tien Wah Press (Pte) Ltd.

CM 11 0 9 8 7 6 5 4 3 2 1

Library and Archives Canada Cataloguing in Publication

Turner, Tracey
         Dreadful fates / written by Tracey Turner ; illustrated by Sally Kindberg.

ISBN 978-1-55453-644-3

1. Death — Juvenile literature. I. Kindberg, Sally II. Title.

HQ1073.3.T87 2011   j306.9   C2010-904211-5

Kids Can Press is a /orus™ Entertainment company

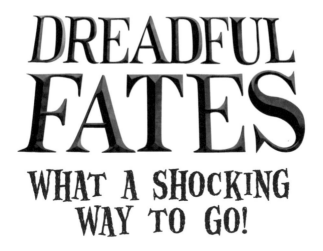

DREADFUL
FATES
WHAT A SHOCKING
WAY TO GO!

WRITTEN BY TRACEY TURNER
ILLUSTRATED BY SALLY KINDBERG

KIDS CAN PRESS

Contents

Introduction

It's a grim thought that we could all meet our final dreadful fate at any time. But, cheer up, it might involve a skydiving tortoise, an inflatable elephant or a flying turnip. As you're about to discover, there are some very strange ways to go, including being ...

- engulfed by a giant wave of molasses

- speared by an icicle

- felled by a plummeting leg of lamb

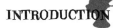

As well as the people who died in unusual ways, there are those who continued their adventures long after death. Find out about ...

- the voyages of Ludwig van Beethoven's skull

- the stuffed cowboy

- the king who ended up as a salt dish

Read on for stories of chocolate coffins, mummified hearts, missing skulls and falling monks in this collection of hundreds of bizarre, puzzling and completely unexpected fates.

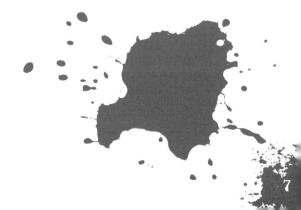

Squashed, Bashed, Speared and Tripped

Dreadful fates can strike in all sorts of different ways: plunging icicles, flying vegetables, blast furnaces and umbrella stands ...

- King Béla I of Hungary died in 1063 when his throne collapsed. There were rumors at the time that the throne's large canopy may have been sabotaged in an attempt to kill the king.

- In east London in 1989, a man died after being hit by a turnip thrown from a passing car.

- In 1991, a woman was driving through a tunnel in Italy when an icicle smashed through the roof of her car and killed her instantly.

- On a nighttime trip to the toilet, first-century Swedish king Fjölnir of Ynglingatal became disoriented and fell into a vat of mead, where he drowned.

Squashed Surgeon

During the Middle Ages, people were superstitious about the huge, ancient stone circle at Avebury in Wiltshire, England, and removed stones, smashed them or toppled them over. Underneath one of them, the skeleton of a man was discovered, possibly a barber-surgeon because of the equipment found with his skeleton. It seems he had been helping to remove one of the ancient stones when it fell on him and crushed him to death. His body had remained under the stone for hundreds of years — it wasn't discovered until 1938. The man's skeleton is now stored in the Natural History Museum in London.

- In 2003, a Scottish woman died when she fell into an open dishwasher and was stabbed by a carving knife.

- Mitchell Falls in North Carolina, U.S., is named after the explorer Elisha Mitchell. In 1857, Elisha Mitchell slipped, fell into the waterfall and died.

- French composer and conductor Jean-Baptiste Lully speared himself through the foot with his conducting staff during an energetic performance. He died months later after the wound had become gangrenous.

- A student in Quebec, Canada, was crushed to death by a vending machine in 1998 when he tried to shake out a free drink. In fact, vending machines have caused thirty-five deaths over the last twenty years.

- Isadora Duncan, a famous American dancer, was fond of wearing long, floaty scarves. In 1927, she was a passenger in a car when her scarf got caught by the tire and strangled her.

- A South African man was killed when a leg of lamb fell on top of him from a third-story window in 1991.

DEATH BY TORTOISE

Aeschylus, the ancient Greek dramatist, died when an eagle dropped a tortoise on his head, according to the Roman historian Pliny. Perhaps this isn't as unlikely as it sounds: Bearded vultures, which look very much like eagles, have been spotted dropping tortoises onto rocks to break their shells. If it *did* happen, it was certainly extremely unlucky — sightings of tortoise-dropping are rare, and there are no other recorded deaths by falling tortoise. Also, according to Pliny, a prediction had been made that Aeschylus would die on that day, but in a different way: A house would fall on him. And that's what happened, if you think of a tortoise's shell as its house. In order to avoid that fate, Aeschylus stayed outdoors that day, only to be flattened by a falling reptile.

Oh!

No!

- The story goes that Holy Roman Emperor Frederick I stopped to drink from a river during the Third Crusade in 1190 and fell headfirst into the water because of the weight of his armor. Unable to get up again, he drowned.

- In 1753, Russian physicist Georg Wilhelm Richmann became the first person to die while carrying out an electrical experiment. He was working during a thunderstorm. Reportedly, the extremely rare weather phenomenon known as "ball lightning" appeared in the room and bashed him in the head, killing him instantly. It also knocked out his assistant and ripped the door off its hinges.

- The ancient Greek philosopher Zeno of Citium, famous for starting the Stoic school of philosophy, died around 262 BC. According to one report of his death, he was on his way home when he tripped and fell, breaking his toe in the process. He saw this as a sign — he was very old, and should do what was appropriate, according to his philosophy. So he strangled himself.

- A driving instructor in Gloucestershire, England, was killed when he arrived at a monastery to give a lesson. He walked under a ladder and was squashed by a falling monk who had been carrying out repairs to the gutters. The monk made a full recovery.

- A clown was driving to a children's party in California, U.S., in 2005 when his giant balloon elephant, Colonel Jumbo, began to inflate on the backseat. It filled the car rapidly, and the clown died in the resulting car crash.

- In New York, U.S., in 2008, a temporary Walmart employee was trampled to death by a crowd of customers who stampeded through the store's doors the second they opened, desperate to get at the sale items.

- French composer Charles-Valentin Alkan was killed either by a bookcase falling on top of him or by becoming trapped beneath an umbrella stand — reports vary.

- Peter Valyi, Hungary's finance minister, tripped while on an official visit to a steelworks in 1973. He pitched headfirst into a blast furnace and died.

- **Run Over by a Rocket**

English Member of Parliament William Huskisson was run over by *Rocket*, the most famous early steam train, at the opening ceremony of the Liverpool and Manchester Railway in 1830. Huskisson crossed the track to speak to the Duke of Wellington as *Rocket* arrived on a parallel track. Unable to get away in time, he suffered a crushed leg and died later the same day.

LETHAL LACES

A woman was crushed to death by her own corset in 1859. The fashion was for women to have tiny waists, so women wore corsets to pull in their middles and make them as small as possible.

This Parisian woman's tight corset gave her a 33 cm (13 in.) waist but also injured her liver and killed her. There are several reports of women being killed by tightly laced corsets during the 1800s.

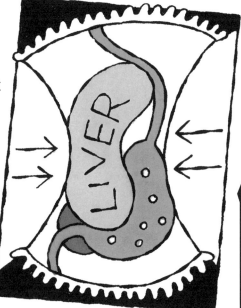

LIVER

13

- Austrian Hans Steininger was famous for his beard: It was 1.4 m (4.6 ft.) long. In 1567, while running away from a fire, he tripped over his beard, broke his neck and died.

- The Irish writer George Bernard Shaw lived to the age of ninety-four, when he fell out of an apple tree he was pruning and died.

- An Australian man was chewing bubble gum as he was driving in 2007. A large bubble burst and stuck to his glasses and face, making him unable to see clearly. He crashed the car and died.

- A Florida ice-cream deliveryman was crushed to death by a load of Nuttie Buddies ice-cream cones.

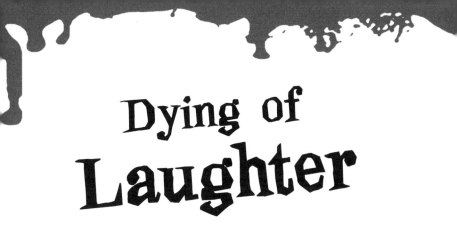

Dying of
Laughter

Surely nothing could be that funny ... yet comedy shows, paintings and even the state of Venice have all proved fatally hilarious.

- In 1410, King Martin of Aragon died of a mixture of uncontrollable laughing and indigestion.

- In 2003, a Thai man died laughing in his sleep. His wife couldn't wake him up, so he never revealed what he found so funny.

- Nanda Bayin, King of Burma, died laughing in 1599 when he was told by a traveling merchant that Venice was a free state with no monarch. He found the idea preposterous and, apparently, hilarious.

- **Royal Joke**

  Scottish writer and royal supporter Thomas Urquhart opposed Oliver Cromwell in the English Civil War and was imprisoned during Cromwell's rule. He is supposed to have died laughing after finding out that Charles II had become King in 1660, ending Cromwell's republic.

- In 1975, a man died laughing at an episode of a sketch comedy TV show called *The Goodies*. The scene he was laughing at showed a Scotsman dressed in a kilt being attacked by a blood sausage, which the Scotsman was trying to fend off with his bagpipes. After the man's death, his wife wrote to the television channel, thanking them for making her husband's last moments so much fun.

- In 1782, a woman died laughing after a production of *The Beggar's Opera*, a humorous musical play. Mrs. Fitzherbert started laughing when a popular actor made his first appearance and, unable to stop, left the theater. She continued laughing until she died the following morning.

- Zeuxis, an ancient Greek artist, is supposed to have died laughing at one of his own paintings. The story goes that an old woman wanted a painting of Aphrodite, the beautiful goddess of love, and insisted that she be used as a model. Zeuxis carried out her wishes but found the result so funny that he couldn't stop laughing and finally choked to death.

HILARIOUS PREDICTION

In Greek legend, the fortune-teller Calchas died laughing because the predicted day of his death had arrived and he wasn't dead. Another soothsayer had told Calchas, who was planting a grapevine, that he would die before he could drink the wine made from the grapes. When the grapes ripened and the wine was made, Calchas invited the soothsayer who had made the prediction to drink a glass with him. As Calchas picked up his glass, the other man repeated his prediction, which caused Calchas to laugh so long and hard that he died.

Bits and Pieces

Skulls, brains and mummified hearts can all go missing after death. And they might turn up in all sorts of unexpected places: on a ship's prow, in cupboards and even on a dinner plate.

- The English poet Percy Bysshe Shelley drowned in a sailing accident off the coast of Italy in 1822. His body washed ashore and was cremated on the beach in a ceremony attended by some of his friends. One of them, Edward Trelawny, rescued Shelley's heart from the flames and gave it to Shelley's wife, Mary, who kept it with her until she died, when it was buried next to her.

- In 1991, four masked thieves made off with the jaw and teeth of Saint Anthony from Saint Francis church in Assisi, Italy.

- King Charles I lost the English Civil War and was beheaded in 1649. His head was sewn back onto his body after his execution so that he could be buried whole. In 1813, the royal surgeon examined Charles I's skeleton and secretly stole one of the bones from Charles's spine. He used the bone as a salt dish to amuse his dinner guests. After many years, Queen Victoria found out and ordered the surgeon to return Charles's bone to the rest of his body.

- In 1586 in York, England, Margaret Clitherow was sentenced to death because of her Catholic religion and for hiding Catholic priests in her house. Her execution was especially horrible — she was crushed to death — and afterwards her body was buried in a garbage dump outside the city walls. Margaret's body was rescued, and some of it is still preserved as a holy relic: Margaret's hand remains in a York convent.

- Juan Perón, the Argentinian president, died in 1974. In 1987, his tomb was desecrated, and thieves made off with his hands as well as some of his personal belongings.

- **Einstein's Brain**

The famous physicist Albert Einstein died in 1955 and, within hours, his brain was removed to find out whether there was anything unusual about it. Dr. Thomas Stoltz Harvey, who had removed and preserved the brain, also removed Einstein's eyes and gave them to an eye specialist. Harvey kept the brain, in two jars filled with formalin, for the next forty years, occasionally sending chunks to specialists around the world. Eventually, after taking the brain on a trip to visit Einstein's granddaughter, Harvey returned the brain to Princeton University's pathology laboratory.

RALEIGH'S HEAD

English explorer and poet Sir Walter Raleigh was found guilty of treason against King James I and beheaded in 1618.

Raleigh's remains were offered to his wife, Elizabeth Throckmorton, who had the body buried but decided to have the head embalmed. She kept it in a leather bag until she died, twenty-nine years later.

Raleigh's head was then passed on to his son, Carew, who looked after it until his own death in 1666. Carew and the head were buried in the tomb containing the rest of Raleigh in Westminster.

But fourteen years later, the head was moved again: Carew's body was dug up, along with Raleigh's head, and moved to a different grave in Surrey.

- Saint Rosalia died near Palermo, Sicily, in 1166, having lived as a hermit in a cave. When a plague came to the area in the 1600s, a hunter claimed to have been visited by Rosalia, who told him that the plague would end if he found her bones in a mountain cave and brought them to Palermo. He did so, and the plague ended. Rosalia's bones are supposed to ward off sickness to this day, even though an examination of the bones in the nineteenth century found them to be those of a goat.

- Simon Sudbury, Archbishop of Canterbury and Bishop of London, was beheaded during the Peasants' Revolt in 1381. His body was buried in Canterbury, but a friend took the head to Saint Gregory's church in Sudbury, Suffolk. Instead of burying it, the vicar put the head in a cupboard in the vestry, where it remains.

- **Beautiful Bones**

In the 1500s, a graveyard in Sedlec in the Czech Republic had become too full. All of the tens of thousands of bodies buried there were dug up and the bones put in a pile inside the chapel in the middle of the graveyard, which could then be used for more burials. In the 1800s, the many thousands of bones that had been dug up centuries earlier were put to an unusual use: as decoration for the chapel interior. The altar is made of bones, plus there is an enormous coat of arms made of bones and a huge chandelier that uses all of the 206 bones in the human body at least once. They are still there today.

• Lord Uxbridge's Leg

Henry Paget, Lord Uxbridge, had his leg badly wounded at the Battle of Waterloo. It had to be amputated above the knee, without anesthetic, by doctors in the village of Waterloo, in a house owned by a Monsieur Paris. After the operation, Paris asked permission to bury the leg in his garden, which was granted. The leg was buried and given a tombstone with a long inscription detailing Lord Uxbridge's heroism. It attracted many visitors, including the King of Prussia. Visitors were also shown the chair in which Lord Uxbridge sat during the amputation, complete with blood stains.

In 1878, Lord Uxbridge's son visited the grave and was horrified to see that the bones had been unearthed and were on display. He demanded the return of his father's leg bones but never got them: The bones were kept hidden for years until the last Monsieur Paris died and his widow found them in his study. She didn't want the bones to cause any further trouble, so she burned them in her central heating boiler.

• Cromwell's Head

Oliver Cromwell got rid of the monarchy in England when he had King Charles I executed in 1649 and became the leader of the English Parliament. When he died in 1658, he was given a grand funeral, and his body was embalmed and buried in Westminster Abbey. Two years later, when the monarchy was restored with King Charles II, Cromwell was dug up and publicly executed. His head was stuck on a pole in London, where it remained for twenty-four years. Then it passed from person to person for centuries, at one point turning up in a freak show labeled as "the monster's head." It wasn't buried until 1960, more than three hundred years after it had been cut off, in the grounds of Cromwell's old college in Cambridge.

DOCTOR DEATH

In the early part of the nineteenth century, Robert Liston was a Scottish surgeon famous for his skill and speed — he was said to be capable of amputating and stitching up a limb in thirty seconds. The story goes that he managed to kill three people during one operation: He cut off the fingers of his assistant, who later died of blood poisoning; he slashed the coat of an observer, who died of fright; and the patient later died of an infection.

Bits and Pieces of Saint John

The prophet John the Baptist was imprisoned by Herod, ruler of Galilee, and beheaded in AD 30. One account says that Herod granted his stepdaughter a wish, and she asked for the head of John the Baptist. After his execution, his body was probably buried in Samaria, and the tomb was later opened and some of the remains burned.

No one knows what really happened to the saint's remains. Today, several different places all claim to have the head of John the Baptist, including Amiens Cathedral in France, the church of San Silvestro in Capite in Rome and the Residenz Museum in Munich, Germany. The saint's right hand is claimed by a monastery in Montenegro and also by another monastery in Greece. The Topkapi Palace in Istanbul claims to have John the Baptist's skull and arm, and so does the Monastery of Saint Macarius the Great in Egypt.

- Mexican revolutionary Francisco "Pancho" Villa was murdered in 1923. His head was stolen three years after his burial, and no one knows what happened to it — one story says it was stolen for an eccentric American millionaire who collected the skulls of famous people. His body was later moved, although there is a rumor that Villa's body was swapped with a different one to thwart future grave robbers. A pawnshop in Texas claims to have Villa's "trigger finger."

GERONIMO'S SKULL

Apache warrior Geronimo was captured by the U.S. army and died at Fort Sill, Oklahoma, in 1909 and was buried there. In the 1980s, one of Geronimo's descendants, Ned Anderson, asked for the warrior's remains to be returned to his homeland in Arizona. Anderson received a letter from a man claiming to be a member of Yale University's Skull and Bones Society, which said that Geronimo's skull and other bones had been stolen from his grave at Fort Sill in a midnight raid by the Society in 1918, and that the skull was now kept in the "Tomb," the clubhouse of the Skull and Bones Society.

One of the thieves was identified as Prescott Bush, father of President George Bush and grandfather of President George W. Bush. Anderson visited the Skull and Bones Society to demand the return of Geronimo's remains, but he was told that although there was a skull referred to as "Geronimo," it wasn't really the Apache warrior's skull. The mystery has never been resolved, but there doesn't seem to be any evidence that Geronimo's grave at Fort Sill was ever disturbed. It might well be that the theft of the skull was a just a story made up by the Skull and Bones Society. In 2009, Geronimo's descendants sued the Skull and Bones Society for the theft of their ancestor's remains.

- General "Stonewall" Jackson died in 1863 during the American Civil War. Several days earlier, his left arm had been badly injured in battle and was amputated. The arm was buried at the battle site, but the rest of General Jackson was buried at Lexington, Virginia. In 1929, the arm was dug up, put in a small box and reburied in the cemetery of a nearby town.

Cut–up Cook

English explorer Captain Cook met his dreadful fate in 1779, when he was attacked and killed by the inhabitants of the Hawaiian Islands. Cook's crew asked the Hawaiians to return their captain's body and, eventually, received a series of grisly packages: First came a parcel containing Cook's thigh, then some bones, the legs minus the feet, the arms, the hands, a skull and a scalp. The crew gave the various bits of Captain Cook a burial at sea, but they never found out what happened to the rest of him.

Oswald's Remains

King Oswald of Northumbria was defeated in battle in AD 642, killed and chopped to pieces. His head, body, arms and legs were displayed on poles in the town of Oswestry. Years later, when Oswald was made a saint, his remains were rescued: His head was put inside the coffin of Saint Cuthbert and moved to Durham Cathedral; an arm ended up in the Church of Saint Oswald in Cumbria; while a Yorkshire monastery claimed to have various bits of Oswald, including an arm. Churches and monasteries all over Europe claimed to have pieces of the saint.

- Queen Anne Boleyn of England was beheaded in 1536. According to one story, her body was put inside an old chest with her head tucked under her arm and buried in the Tower of London. Another story suggests that her heart was stolen and hidden in Suffolk, where it was found in 1836 in a church wall and reburied in Saint Peter and Paul Church, Salle, Norfolk.

- The assassin of U.S. president James Garfield, Charles Guiteau, was hanged for his crime in 1882. Some of Guiteau's brain is displayed in a Philadelphia museum, while another piece of it, together with some of his bones and some of James Garfield's, are stored at the National Museum of Health and Medicine in Washington, D.C.

- ## Nicholas Nicked

  Saint Nicholas died in AD 326 and his bones were kept in the crypt of a church in Myra, Turkey. In 1087, a band of sailors stole the bones and took them to Bari, Italy, where people still visit him today. When the tomb was opened in the 1950s for repairs, it was discovered that some of the bones had gone missing. Other European churches claim to have bits of Saint Nicholas — an arm bone in Rimini, Italy, a tooth in Corbie, France, and finger bones scattered around France and Germany.

- Vlad the Impaler, the Prince of Wallachia, was well known for his cruel punishments. He was killed in battle in 1476, after which his Turkish opponents beheaded the body and sent Vlad's head to the Turkish Sultan in Istanbul, where it was displayed on a stake.

- Mata Hari was convicted of espionage in France and condemned to death by firing squad. After her death in 1917, her body was used for medical study, and her head was embalmed and kept in the Museum of Anatomy in Paris. In 2000, it was discovered that Mata Hari's head was missing, and probably had been for many years. Its whereabouts remains a mystery.

- At an auction in England in 2005, someone paid £11 000 (US $14 500) for one of the French emperor Napoleon's teeth, which had been removed while he was in exile on Saint Helena.

REVOLUTIONARY MUMMY

After he died in 1924, Russian revolutionary Vladimir Lenin's brain was removed so that it could be examined for evidence of his genius.

Scientist Oskar Vogt spent two and a half years studying the brain and concluded that particular neurons were more numerous and larger than most people's.

genius?

Lenin's body was mummified and is still on public display in Moscow, although there is some controversy over whether Lenin is a true mummy or, at least partly, a waxwork. In recent years, there have been several proposals to remove the body from public display and bury it.

GRUESOME BOOK COVERS

The skin of hanged criminals has sometimes ended up as book covers. In 1821, John Horwood was hanged at Bristol, England, his body was dissected and the skin and skeleton were prepared by the Royal Infirmary's chief surgeon. A book about Horwood's trial, execution and dissection was bound in Horwood's skin — it remains in Bristol's Royal Infirmary along with Horwood's preserved skeleton.

William Corder was hanged in 1828 for murder, and a book about his trial and execution, bound in his skin, is in the public library at Bury St. Edmunds, England.

William Burke and William Hare were body snatchers who murdered people in order to sell the dead bodies for medical research. They were both caught, and William Burke was hanged for his crimes in Edinburgh, Scotland, in 1829. His body was dissected in public at the Edinburgh Medical College, where his skeleton and a book covered in his skin are still kept.

Someone Else's Head

Petrarch, the Italian poet, died in 1374. In 2003, his body was dug up in order to make an accurate reconstruction of the poet's face using his skull, but scientists discovered that the skull and the rest of the skeleton belonged to two different people. While the body does seem to be Petrarch's, the skull is *not* his and probably belongs to a woman who died before Petrarch was born. In 1630, a gang of thieves led by a friar broke into Petrarch's tomb and stole some bones, but it does not seem that the skull was taken on this occasion — the hole they made wasn't big enough for the skull to be removed. The search for an explanation continues.

- Pompey, the ancient Roman general, went to war with his old ally Julius Caesar. He was murdered in Egypt, and his head was cut off and presented to Caesar in a basket.

- In 1305, Scottish leader William Wallace was hanged, drawn and quartered after he was defeated by the English. His body was divided up and sent to various parts of England and Scotland as a warning to traitors. Different bits of him ended up in Newcastle, Berwick, Perth and Stirling, and his head was stuck on a pole on London Bridge.

- The English writer D.H. Lawrence died in Vence, France, in 1930 and was buried there. Five years later, his remains were unearthed and burned. Lawrence's widow arranged for her boyfriend to pick up the ashes and bring them to Taos, New Mexico, where they lived. The ashes were brought to Taos in an urn and mixed with cement to make a shrine for Lawrence. Later, the boyfriend confessed he had dumped the ashes near Marseilles in France and filled the urn with cigarette ash.

MUSICAL SKULLS

Austrian composer Franz Joseph Haydn died in 1809 and was given a grand funeral and buried in the Hundsthurmer graveyard. Eleven years later, Haydn's body was dug up and reburied elsewhere, but his head was discovered to be missing. A skull was sent anonymously and buried with Haydn's body, but it turned out that it belonged to someone else. Haydn's real head was given to the Society of Friends of Music in Vienna. It was buried in 1954, at last reunited with Haydn's body.

Wolfgang Amadeus Mozart died in 1791 and was buried in a mass grave. Ten years later, the grave was opened, and the famous composer's skull was identified by the grave digger, who gave it to a friend. After several changes of hands, it ended up at the International Mozarteum Foundation in Salzburg, Austria, in 1901. For the next fifty-three years, the skull was on public display and although it's hidden from view now, the skull remains at the Foundation. The story goes that staff members at the Foundation have heard musical notes, screams and other noises coming from the skull. However, no one knows whether it really is Mozart's despite several recent tests.

The German composer Ludwig van Beethoven died in 1827. The doctor who performed an autopsy the following day broke the skull into various pieces. In 1863, the Society of Friends of Music in Vienna dug Beethoven up, together with the composer Schubert, for reburial in Währing Cemetery, and at this point some of Beethoven's skull escaped. It seems that the director of the Society of Friends of Music kept various fragments of the skull, which he then passed on to Dr. Seligmann at the University of Vienna, who kept a collection of skulls. Dr. Seligmann died in 1892, and Beethoven's skull passed to various of his descendants over the following century until they ended up with a man who brought the skull bones to his home in California. Eventually, the Center for Beethoven Studies, also in California, tracked down the bones and now keeps them. Tests were carried out that revealed Beethoven had suffered from lead poisoning for years before his death.

FRENCH HEARTS

Louis XIV of France died in 1715, and his heart was buried separately from his body, which was the tradition at the time for French royalty. During the French Revolution, the tomb containing his embalmed heart was wrecked and the heart stolen. The heart was sold to Lord Harcourt, who sold it to William Buckland, the Dean of Westminster. Buckland was famous for eating all sorts of uncommon food including alligator and pickled horse tongue. The story goes that one night he ate Louis XIV's heart for dinner.

After the French Revolution, King Louis XVI and Queen Marie Antoinette were imprisoned along with their son, the uncrowned Louis XVII. The King and Queen were executed, and the boy died in prison of tuberculosis in 1795. A doctor removed his heart, according to the tradition, smuggled it out of the prison, pickled it in alcohol and stored it in a vase in his library. It was stolen by a student, who eventually gave it back, and the heart had various owners over the years, including the Spanish royal family, who returned it to Paris in 1975. It's been stored at the Basilica of Saint Denis near Paris ever since, although there were doubts as to whose heart it really was. In 2004, DNA tests revealed that it almost certainly was the heart of Louis XVII, and it was placed in the royal crypt in Saint Denis the same year.

- Henry Grey, First Duke of Suffolk, was the father of Lady Jane Grey, whom he supported in a bid to become Queen of England. He was beheaded for treason in 1554. In 1851, a mummified head in a box, thought to be Henry Grey's, was found in a church near the Tower of London and placed in a glass box by the vicar. (Some of the nose was broken off during handling.) The head was later moved to Saint Botolph's, Aldgate, where it remains.

- Sir Thomas More was beheaded for treason in 1535, and his headless body was buried in the Tower of London. More's head was boiled and displayed on a pole on London Bridge. His daughter, Margaret Roper, bribed the bridge keeper and took the head home. More's head was put on display in St. Dunstan's church, Canterbury, for many years.

- **Unwilling Exhibit**

Eighteenth-century surgeon John Hunter dissected dead human bodies and experimented on them, and he sometimes robbed graves in order to get new specimens. He was particularly keen to have the body of Charles Byrne, known as the Irish Giant, who was nearly 2.5 m (8 ft.) tall. While Byrne was still alive, the surgeon offered him money in return for his body when he died. Byrne refused. But when Byrne died, John Hunter arranged to steal his body from its coffin and replace it with stones. Charles Byrne's body is still on display at the Hunterian Museum at the Royal College of Surgeons, in London, England.

- According to legend, the infamous pirate Blackbeard was wounded twenty-five times before he finally died at the hands of British troops. British lieutenant Maynard then cut off Blackbeard's head and stuck it on the prow of his ship.

• Heavy Head

Ancient Roman politician Gaius Gracchus was made an "enemy of Rome" by his opponents. One of them, Opimius, offered a reward in return for Gracchus's head: the weight of the head in gold. According to a Roman historian, Gracchus was killed by his servant, who then killed himself. Because of the reward, another man cut off Gracchus's head, scooped out the brains and filled the skull with molten lead. When the lead hardened, he took it to Opimius to be weighed, and was paid in full.

• Goya, the Spanish painter, died in 1828 in France and was buried in Bordeaux. In 1901, his body was brought back to Spain, but it was discovered that the painter was not alone: Inside his coffin were two skeletons — and only one head. Apparently, Goya had asked for his skull to be hidden because he didn't agree with the current fashion for examining skulls. He had been buried alongside a relative, which accounts for the odd number of skeletons and skulls. Goya is now buried with his companion, but without his head, in San Antonio de la Florida church in Madrid.

- After his assassination in 1865, U.S. president Abraham Lincoln was embalmed and sent on a grand tour of the country so that people could pay their respects. When he was finally buried, his coffin had to be moved because of threats to steal the body. In fact, Abraham Lincoln has been dug up and reburied seventeen times over the years, and his coffin was opened five times to make sure the corpse was his.

- The English writer Thomas Hardy died in 1928, and his body was buried in Poet's Corner in Westminster Abbey. Because Hardy had wanted to be buried with his wife in a grave in Dorset, the decision was made to remove his heart and bury that in the Dorset grave. The story goes that Hardy's housekeeper left the heart on the kitchen table, where it was eaten by the cat, so a pig's heart took its place in the grave.

- In Cardiganshire, Wales, is the grave of a leg. The gravestone reads

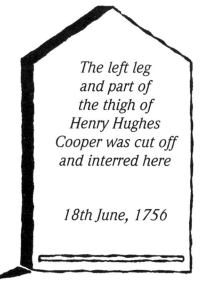

The left leg and part of the thigh of Henry Hughes Cooper was cut off and interred here

18th June, 1756

Henry Hughes Cooper later left Wales (with his remaining leg) for America. The grave inspired poet John Ormond to write "Lament for a Leg."

- Henrietta Maria, wife of Charles I of England, died in 1669, and her body was buried in a French cathedral, except for her heart, which was buried in a convent at Chaillot. During the French Revolution, the convent was ransacked, and the heart went missing.

- In Pinewood Cemetery, Florida, U.S., is the elaborate marble and stained-glass tomb of Dr. Adler Rawlings, who died in 1948. A group of local teenagers made the tomb their favorite place to hang out and used the coffin as a card table. One day, they decided to open the coffin. They took out the skeleton and played golf using the leg bones and skull. The following day the police arrived. Dr. Rawlings's remains were replaced in the tomb, which was sealed with concrete, although the skull was never recovered.

Fatal Food

We all know there are certain things you shouldn't eat: toxic fish, molten gold and poisonous fungi among them. But cherries and milk could also prove fatal — and, of course, so could being eaten.

- King Henry I of England died in 1135 after eating too many lampreys — a parasitic, eel-like fish and a very popular dish in medieval times.

- Ancient Roman leader Crassus was extremely rich. He was defeated in battle in Parthia and sent to the Parthian king. According to some reports, the king had Crassus killed by having molten gold poured down his throat because of his greed for money. There's a story that his head was then cut off and used as a prop in a play performed for the Parthian king.

- Poisonous mushrooms are notoriously difficult to tell from edible ones, which has been useful to poisoners throughout history. One of the most famous victims is probably Roman emperor Claudius, who was very likely poisoned by his wife with a dish of mushrooms.

- According to legend, François Vatel, Louis XIV's chef, killed himself rather than face the shame of keeping the French king waiting for his dinner when a seafood order was late to arrive. His body was discovered by the messenger sent to tell him of its arrival.

FISH FOOD

Pufferfish, or *fugu* as it's known in Japan, is a dangerous dish because the liver and some other parts of the fish are highly poisonous, and a tiny amount is enough to kill a human. Fugu chefs have to train for years before they are allowed to prepare the dish in restaurants. But Japanese actor Bando Mitsugoro VIII claimed that he was immune to the poison and ate four helpings of the dish. The fugu poisoned the actor, and he died. The chef who prepared the food lost his license. Today, preparation of fugu is carefully controlled, and deaths are extremely rare, although in the 1950s, there were more than 150 deaths in a single year due to badly prepared fugu.

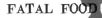

- The twelfth president of the United States, Zachary Taylor, drank lots of iced milk and ate an enormous pile of cherries one hot Fourth of July. He became ill with indigestion and died five days later. There were rumors that the president might have been poisoned, and finally, in the 1990s, more than 140 years after his death, Taylor's body was dug up and examined. The results showed that the president hadn't been poisoned — he had just eaten too much.

- Tycho Brahe, Danish nobleman and astronomer, is thought to have died because he was too polite to leave a banquet table. Although he needed to go to the bathroom, it would have been extremely bad manners to leave the table before the meal was over, so Brahe sat where he was until he strained his bladder. It is believed that this caused his death, although it is not certain — he might have been murdered by a rival or suffered from lead poisoning.

- In 1814, there was an accident at Meux and Company Brewery in central London, England. 1.5 million L (0.4 million gal.) of beer gushed out of the vats and into the surrounding streets, destroying two buildings and killing nine people.

- In Boston, U.S., in 1919, at the Purity Distilling Company, a huge tank of molasses burst. The sticky molasses formed a wave several meters (feet) high, which went rushing through the streets and killed twenty-one people and several horses.

- The story goes that the Roman emperor Elagabalus, who ruled during the third century, killed his dinner guests by dropping thousands of rose petals into the room at a banquet. The rose petals smothered them to death.

Hic

Urk

Cucumber King

The story goes that Theinhko, King of Burma in AD 931, ate some cucumbers he saw growing in a field. He had not asked permission from the farmer, who was furious and beat Theinhko to death with his spade. The queen was worried that there would be a revolt when people found out that the king had been killed, and perhaps she hadn't liked him much anyway, so she smuggled the farmer into the palace to take the place of the king and kept quiet about the killing. Later, the cucumber farmer was crowned King Nyaung-u Sawrahan of Burma. He became known as "the Cucumber King."

- King Adolph Frederick of Sweden died in 1771 after eating an enormous dinner including caviar, lobster and champagne, and no fewer than fourteen helpings of his favorite dessert.

- French explorer Marion du Fresne and twenty-six others in his group became the first European victims of cannibalism in New Zealand when they were killed, cooked and eaten in 1772.

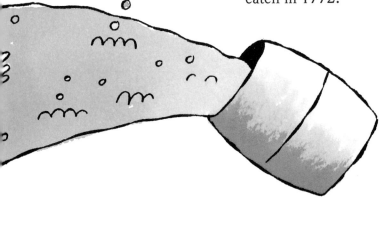

Animal Encounters

Lions and tigers, venomous snakes, elephants, monkeys, poodles ... the animal kingdom is out to get us.

- Victorian botanist David Douglas was studying plants in Hawaii when he fell into a pit dug as a trap for wild cattle. Apparently, he died when a bull fell in on top of him, or possibly when an angry bull that was already in the pit trampled him to death. Murder (by an ex-convict cattle farmer, not the bull) was suspected, but never proved.

- Viking leader Ragnar Hairy-Breeches was defeated in battle by King Aelle II of Northumberland in AD 865. Aelle ordered his execution: Ragnar was thrown into a pit of venomous snakes.

- In 2007, a Kenyan man was attacked by a lion but managed to kill it with his spear. He staggered off, badly injured, only to be set upon by a pack of hyenas. He finally made it to a road, where he was picked up by a motorist and taken to a hospital, but sadly he died of his injuries.

- A U.S. tourist on safari in Tanzania in 2001 left the safari vehicle in order to take a photograph of the local wildlife. She was quickly trampled by an elephant.

- King Minrekyawsa of Burma was crushed to death by his elephant in 1417. Only six years later, King Razadarit of Burma became entangled in a rope he was using to lasso an elephant and died.

- King Alexander I of Greece died in 1920 after being attacked by monkeys. He was trying to defend his pet dog from them.

- The deputy mayor of Delhi died after being attacked by a group of wild monkeys in 2007.

- Roman emperor Titus is supposed to have died because an insect flew up his nose and gnawed on his brain — after being gnawed at for seven years, Titus died.

- In South Africa in 2005, a pickpocket was running away from an angry crowd and climbed over a high fence to escape. He was in Bloemfontein Zoo and hadn't realized he was climbing into the tiger enclosure, where he was soon mauled to death.

- According to legend, ancient Greek dramatist Euripides was set upon and killed by a pack of hunting dogs while staying with the Macedonian king — some versions of the story say the dogs were deliberately let loose. Another story says he was torn apart by a group of women who were furious at how he portrayed female characters in his plays.

- In India in 1981, a man died when a bird of prey dropped a live viper on his head — the snake bit him. The bird came back for the viper and flew away with it.

- In 1995, six people in Egypt drowned trying to rescue a chicken from a well. The chicken survived.

- Malaysian Ali Khan Sumsadin spent twenty-one days living in a glass box with six thousand scorpions, and forty days living with venomous snakes. He died in 2006 when he was bitten by a king cobra.

- Timothy Treadwell spent every summer for thirteen years living with grizzly bears in Alaska. In 2003, he and his girlfriend were both killed by a grizzly, and he was partly eaten.

- A man died in 2006 when a flying kangaroo hit his car in Western Australia. The kangaroo had been hit by another car and became airborne before it crashed through the windshield of the second car.

- Catfish rarely become man-eaters, but three people were killed between 1998 and 2007 by goonch catfish in the Kali River on the India–Nepal border.

- A pack of wolves found their way into the city and killed forty people in Paris in the winter of 1450. Eventually, Parisians lured the wolves to the gates of Notre Dame Cathedral, where they surrounded and killed them.

- In 1988, a poodle called Cachi fell from a thirteenth-floor balcony in Buenos Aires and landed on an elderly woman, killing them both instantly. There was a third victim of the incident. A woman in the crowd that had gathered was knocked down by a bus and killed.

- The world-record holder for spending the most time in a container with snakes was Thailand's Boonreung Bauchan. In 2004, he was bitten by a cobra and died.

- Egyptian king Menes was killed by a hippopotamus around 3100 BC, after reigning for sixty-two years.

- The Reverend Harold Davidson, a disgraced priest, performed with a lion called Freddy, proclaiming his innocence of the charges brought against him by the Church of England. One day in 1937, Freddy mauled him and Davidson died soon afterward.

- In a single zoo in Kent, England, three keepers have been killed by tigers and one crushed to death by an elephant.

- In 2001, Mary Aristides, a member of the criminal underworld in Greece, was on her way to plant a homemade bomb, which she had put by the hand brake in her car. Her dog, a Rottweiler called Boris, sat on it. It exploded, killing them both.

- ## Tyger Fierce

Hannah Twynnoy was a barmaid in a Wiltshire town in 1703. Her gravestone carries an unusual epitaph:

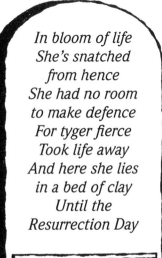

*In bloom of life
She's snatched
from hence
She had no room
to make defence
For tyger fierce
Took life away
And here she lies
in a bed of clay
Until the
Resurrection Day*

She really *was* killed by a tiger. Apparently, a circus was set up on the grounds of the pub where she worked. In those days, trained wild animals were a feature of some circus acts. Although she'd been warned not to, Hannah liked to tease the tiger. One day, it broke loose and mauled her to death, making her the first recorded person to be killed by a tiger in Britain.

- John Russell, the twelfth Duke of Bedford, was very fond of budgies. In 1953, while aiming at a bird of prey that was posing a threat to his birds, he accidentally shot and killed himself.

- The writer Edgar Allan Poe died in 1849 under mysterious circumstances. He was found on the streets of Baltimore, U.S., having had some sort of fit and wearing someone else's clothes. He died at the hospital a few days later. The widely accepted theory was that he had had too much to drink, but the latest theory suggests that he had been bitten by a rabid animal: In his last days at the hospital, his symptoms were very similar to the final stages of rabies.

Unusual Funerals and Curious Coffins

Most people would like an appropriate send-off. For some, this involves blasting into space, being turned into a diamond or burial in a chocolate coffin.

- In 1724, Maggie Dickson was hanged in Edinburgh, Scotland. As her coffin was carried away, people heard banging noises from inside it. The coffin was opened, and Maggie was found to be alive. If Maggie had been hanged in England, she would have been taken straight back to the gallows and hanged until dead, but under Scottish law, she was allowed to go free. She became known as Half Hangit Maggie and lived for another forty years, running a pub.

- A Swedish candy salesman was buried in a chocolate coffin in 1973.

- King John of England was accused of being a werewolf during his lifetime. After he died and was buried, monks complained of howling noises coming from his tomb. His body was dug up and moved so the monks would not be disturbed.

- Unusual headstones are becoming more popular in the Western world. They include a granite Newcastle United soccer jersey, a car, a lightbulb and a game of Scrabble.

- King George IV of England's coffin was only just big enough. When the coffin began to expand from the pressure of trapped gases and threatened to explode, holes had to be drilled in the sides.

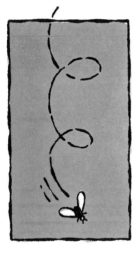

- A French undertaker was killed when a pile of coffins fell on top of him in 1982. He was buried in one of them.

- Journalist Hunter S. Thompson died in 2005. His cremated remains were blasted into the sky in a spectacular fireworks display.

- The ancient Roman poet Virgil staged an enormous and expensive funeral for his "pet" housefly, complete with an orchestra, pallbearers and eulogies, at his grand villa in Rome. The ceremony meant that Virgil's land could be classified as a cemetery, and therefore he didn't have to pay tax on it.

Virgil's "pet"

- American general Anthony Wayne has two graves. He was buried in Pennsylvania, then, years later, his son decided that the general should be buried at the family plot. The body was dug up, dissected and boiled to  separate the flesh from the bones, then the skeleton was taken to the family burial plot. The rest of the gruesome remains, plus the doctor's knives, were reburied in the old grave.

- Rodrigo Borgia, who became Pope Alexander VI, died in Rome in 1503. His body rotted very quickly because of the hot weather and became black, smelly and very swollen. The carpenters who made the coffin had a lot of trouble stuffing the body inside it. Because of the terrible state of his body, no one could believe that the Pope had died from natural causes and thought he must have been poisoned — although he probably died of the disease malaria.

- Alexander Douglas, Duke of Hamilton, Scotland, lived to an old age and became obsessed with finding a grand tomb for himself. He bought an ancient Egyptian sarcophagus but found that he was too tall for it. When he died in 1825, he was embalmed and placed inside the sarcophagus, but his feet had to be cut off and put in separately.

- King Henry V of England died in France. His body was boiled to separate the flesh from the bones, then the skeleton was sent back to England to be buried.

- When Martin Van Butchell's wife died in 1775, he had her embalmed, gave her glass eyes, dressed her in a lace dress and put her in a glass coffin in his living room, referring to her as "my dear departed." Eventually, Van Butchell remarried and, at his second wife's request, moved the remains of his first wife to the Royal College of Surgeons of England, where they were eventually destroyed during the Second World War.

ALEXANDER'S TOMB

After a lot of conquering, Alexander the Great died in 323 BC when he was thirty-three years old. He might have died of malaria or because he'd been drinking too much, or he might have been poisoned by an enemy — or even his wife. One story says that his body was embalmed in honey, then placed in a glass coffin, while other reports say his body was put in a golden coffin.

For centuries, Alexander's body was displayed in his tomb in Alexandria, the capital city of Egypt at the time, where it was visited by several Roman emperors. Emperor Augustus accidentally broke Alexander's nose when he kissed the embalmed corpse, and Emperor Caligula stole Alexander's breastplate. Over the years, Alexander's resting place became lost and remains a mystery today.

- Englishman James Lowther, Earl of Lonsdale, had a girlfriend who died young. He had her body embalmed and placed in a glass coffin, which he used as a sideboard in his dining room.

- A tradition of unusually shaped coffins, symbolizing some aspect of the dead person, has grown up in Ghana. You can be buried in almost anything: a rocket, a lobster, a bottle of Coke, a shoe and a chicken are all recent examples.

- In 1977, Sandra West was buried in Texas in her Ferrari car, wearing her favorite nightgown. She and the car were put inside a large box, which was then covered in concrete and buried.

- Reuben John Smith of New York was buried in 1899 in a reclining leather chair, wearing a hat and coat, and with a checkerboard in front of him (in case he got bored). Inside his coat pocket was the key to the tomb (in case he recovered).

- Legend has it that the conqueror Attila the Hun was buried along with some of his treasure in an elaborate coffin underneath the river Tisza in AD 453. His men diverted the course of a section of the river and buried the coffin in the riverbed. To make sure they kept the exact place a secret, they were killed on their return from the burial.

BURIED ALIVE

Before the 1900s, many people were afraid of being buried alive, since diagnosing death used to be more difficult than it is today. Gruesome stories of live burials were common, and some certainly did happen. The Victorian writer and Member of Parliament Lord Lytton asked that his heart be pierced after his death to ensure that he really was dead. Various people paid their doctors to perform similar tasks, such as severing a major artery. Some had contraptions installed in their coffins so that they could signal to the outside world if they woke up and found themselves buried, often using a bell. In 1896, the London Society for the Prevention of Premature Burial was formed.

- William the Conqueror, King of England, died in 1087. His body was too big for the coffin and had to be forced into it, which made the body leak. It smelled so bad that some of the people at his funeral ran from the church holding their noses, while the priests rushed through the funeral service. His tomb was opened twice in later centuries: during the 1500s, when William's bones were scattered throughout the town of Caen, and again during the French Revolution, when even more of the skeleton went missing. Today, only a thigh bone remains.

- **Brazilian Freud de Melo completed his own burial chamber in 2008 — it comes complete with food, water, TV, air supply and a megaphone for communicating to the outside world, due to the man's fear of being buried alive.**

- Silent film comic Charlie Chaplin died in 1977. Soon afterward, his body was stolen from his grave and a large ransom demanded from his family. They refused to pay, and the body was found eleven weeks later. Charlie Chaplin's body was reburied in a more secure coffin.

- Ed Headrick, inventor of the Frisbee, died in 2002. He asked for his ashes to be incorporated into a series of special edition Frisbees, "Steady Ed's Memorial Discs," which are available to buy from the Disc Golf Association.

- Gene Roddenberry, creator of the television series *Star Trek*, was sent into space after his death: Some of his ashes were put on the space shuttle *Columbia*. More of his ashes are planned to be launched into space in 2012. James Doohan, the actor who played Scotty in *Star Trek*, also had his ashes sent into space.

ashes inside

- Queen Victoria died in 1901. Her body was displayed in the dining room of her home on the Isle of Wight, Osborne House, for ten days, before being taken to London for another few days of being displayed and finally buried. Despite the fact that she had dressed in black mourning clothes for nearly forty years following the death of her husband, Victoria banned black at her own funeral — white and purple were used instead.

Preserved in a Biscuit Tin

Queen Victoria's son-in-law, Henry of Battenberg, died of malaria while he was in Africa in 1896. His body was carried by ship on the long journey back to England. Hot weather and the length of the trip meant that Henry's body began to rot. Various unsuccessful attempts at preserving the body were made. Finally, a coffin was cobbled together from biscuit tins, and Henry's body was preserved in rum until it reached England and could be buried.

- In Europe in the Middle Ages, rich people would pay for their bodies to be taken apart and various bits buried in different places. People believed that if your body parts were sent to different monasteries and churches, you would have more people praying for the salvation of your soul and a greater chance of getting into heaven.

- Alexander T. Stewart, a rich U.S. businessman, died in 1876. Shortly after his burial, his body was stolen and held for ransom. Mrs. Stewart paid $20 000 to get it back. Her husband was reburied in a tomb fitted with an early form of burglar alarm.

- Because of the demand for dead bodies for medical research in the eighteenth and nineteenth centuries, criminals known as "body snatchers" or "resurrection men" would dig up freshly buried bodies and sell them to surgeons. Impenetrable coffins began to be constructed, made of metal with special fastenings to prevent opening. Some were even booby-trapped with explosive devices.

- The poet and painter Dante Gabriel Rossetti buried some of his poems with his wife. Several years later, he regretted burying them and, in 1869, he had his wife's coffin dug up so that he could retrieve the poems, which he then had published.

- Instead of being buried or cremated, you could donate your body to the University of Tennessee Anthropology Research Facility. Every year, more than a hundred bodies are donated to the open-air facility, where bodies are left to decompose in various situations — buried, exposed, placed in water, inside body bags or even in car trunks. They are used for teaching and research and, when the bodies have rotted away completely, the skeletons are collected and used for research, too.

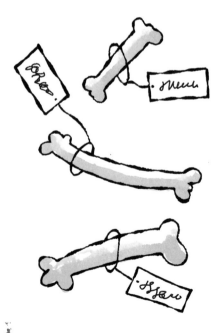

- Philip I of Castile, known as Philip the Handsome, died suddenly in 1506. His wife, Joanna the Mad, refused to have his body buried and kept it in a coffin by her side at all times.

- A glassblower in London was commissioned to make an eggtimer for someone's cremated remains.

- Queen Catherine of Valois, wife of King Henry V of England, died in 1437 and was buried in Westminster Abbey. Some years later, the lid of her tomb became displaced, revealing her body, which became a gruesome tourist attraction. In a diary entry in 1669, Samuel Pepys records kissing Queen Catherine's corpse on a visit to Westminster Abbey. Queen Catherine was not properly reburied until the nineteenth century.

CLOCK COFFIN

English eccentric Hannah Beswick was terrified of being buried alive. She left £25 000 (US $38 200) in her will to her doctor, on the condition that her body should not be buried and that he should visit her regularly after her death. After she died in 1758, the doctor had Hannah embalmed and kept her in a grandfather clock. He paid her a visit once a year, even though, having been embalmed, she was definitely dead. After the doctor's death in 1813, Hannah Beswick's body was moved to the Manchester Museum of Natural History until 1868, when it was finally buried.

Died in Action

Death can strike at the most inconvenient moments: on stage, on horseback or on an especially bad day in the factory ...

- Martha Mansfield, an American actress, died in 1923 on a film set. She was wearing a Civil War costume that included a large, hooped skirt with ruffles, which caught fire when a careless member of the cast threw away the match he had used to light his cigarette.

- Philetas of Cos, an ancient Greek philosopher and poet, is supposed to have died from lack of sleep because he couldn't stop puzzling over a philosophical problem known as the "liar paradox." The liar paradox involves reasoning about a "liar sentence" such as, "This sentence is false," and the impossibility of deciding its truth.

- In 1981, a Japanese factory worker died when a robot pushed him into a grinding machine at a Kawasaki factory.

- During a soccer match in the Democratic Republic of Congo in 1998, every player on the visiting team was killed by lightning. The home team remained unharmed. It's thought that the metal studs in the players' soccer cleats were to blame.

- In 1994, a Mexican mouth organist choked to death on "the world's smallest mouth organ."

- In a New York horse race in 1953, Sweet Kiss was the first horse to cross the finishing line. Unfortunately, he was carrying a dead jockey, who had died of a heart attack during the race.

- A live television play was on air in 1958 when one of the actors, Gareth Jones, died in between scenes while having his makeup applied. The director continued with the play, improvising around the absence of one of his cast members.

- Actor and comedian Dick Shawn had a heart attack and died on stage in 1987 in San Diego — for some time, the audience assumed it was part of the show.

HOUDINI'S LAST ACT

Famous American magician and escapologist Harry Houdini boasted that he could withstand any blow to the stomach. After a performance one day, a student came into his dressing room and asked if this were true. When Houdini replied that it was, the student punched him repeatedly, although Houdini hadn't had time to prepare his stomach muscles for the blows.

Houdini had been suffering from appendicitis for some time, although he had refused treatment for it, and it's not known whether the punches burst his appendix or whether it would have burst anyway. Despite a high fever and a great deal of pain, Houdini went on with his next performance. He passed out during the course of his show but continued with it after being revived. He was finally taken to hospital after the performance, where he died two days later.

- Opera singer Leonard Warren had a heart attack and died on stage in 1960 during a performance of *La Forza del Destino* (*The Force of Destiny*).

- A man in Michigan, U.S., belonged to the same bowling team for nearly forty-five years. In 2008, he played his first-ever perfect game, high-fived his teammates and suffered a fatal heart attack.

- A young man died of a heart attack in 1981 after playing Berzerk, a robot-shooting video game — it was the first known death related to a video game. The following year, another young man scored two high scores on Berzerk before he also suffered a fatal heart attack.

- In 1979, a man died at the Ford Motor Company, Michigan, U.S., when a robot picking up car parts hit him in the head. He was the first person ever to be killed by a robot.

- The French actor and playwright Molière suffered from tuberculosis and collapsed on stage in a violent fit of coughing. Ironically, he was playing the character of a hypochondriac in his play *The Imaginary Invalid*. He died the same day.

- In 1984, one of Britain's best loved comedians, Tommy Cooper, had a heart attack and died on stage during a televised variety show.

- American Captain John Kendrick was killed on board his ship in the Hawaiian Islands in 1794 when a British ship fired a salute. Unfortunately, the British hadn't realized the cannon was loaded.

- Fitness expert Jim Fixx wrote *The Complete Book of Running*, which made jogging popular in the 1970s. He died in 1984, aged fifty-two, of a heart attack while running.

- In 2005, a Korean man died after playing the computer game StarCraft for fifty hours nonstop.

Murders and Executions

Boiling in butter, drowning in a wine barrel — people have come up with some horrible ways of killing other people. Then there are the ones who simply refuse to die ...

- Hypatia of Alexandria, mathematician and philosopher, was murdered in AD 415 by a group of angry Christians who didn't like her ideas. One gruesome report of her death says that her skin was scraped off with oyster shells.

- Transylvanian countess Elizabeth Báthory was walled up in her own castle as a punishment for murder. She was given food through a small opening in the castle wall, but she eventually died after four years.

- The story goes that in 1222, Adam, Bishop of Caithness, was boiled to death in butter in his own kitchen by an angry crowd made furious by his tax demands.

- Alexius II Comnenus, Byzantine Emperor, was strangled with a bowstring in 1183 on the orders of his co-emperor.

- George Plantagenet, Duke of Clarence, plotted against his brother King Edward IV of England. When he was sentenced to death, he chose the method of his own execution: He was drowned in a barrel of wine.

DEATH BY UMBRELLA

In 1978, a Bulgarian man, Georgi Markov, was stabbed in the leg with an umbrella while waiting for a bus. He developed a fever and died a few days later. Doctors discovered a tiny pellet containing traces of poison embedded in Markov's leg wound. Markov had been critical of the communist regime and was assassinated because of it, although no one has ever been charged for the murder.

INDESTRUCTIBLE RASPUTIN

Russian mystic Rasputin proved very difficult to kill. In 1916, he was invited to a party by Prince Felix Yusupov, who planned to assassinate him with a group of accomplices. First, Rasputin was given cakes and wine that had been poisoned, but he didn't seem to be affected. When they realized this, someone shot him in the chest. The Prince approached Rasputin to check that he was dead, but Rasputin sat up and tried to throttle him.

Rasputin managed to leave the palace, but he was discovered by his murderers crawling toward the gate. They shot him again, beat him up, then bound his hands and feet and threw him into an icy river, where he finally died. Rasputin's body was buried, but the following year, during the February Revolution, a mob dug up the corpse and burned it. The story goes that the body appeared to sit up in the flames.

• Insurance Policy

In the 1930s, a group of five men, later known as the Murder Trust, took out a life insurance policy on a homeless man in order to collect the money when he died. The man was almost always drunk, so the Trust kept feeding him free alcohol at a bar owned by one of the gang in the hope that he would soon die of alcohol poisoning. The man didn't die, even after the gang fed him antifreeze instead of whiskey.

Finally, the Trust got the man drunk, ran him over in a car a few times and left him for dead. Two weeks later, the homeless man reappeared at the bar, explaining that he'd been in the hospital after an accident. Eventually, the gang gassed the man, and at last he died. The Murder Trust members were finally caught and sent to prison, and four of them were executed.

- In 44 BC, Julius Caesar was assassinated by twelve of his fellow ancient Roman politicians, who were waiting for him with knives hidden under their togas. He was stabbed twenty-three times. A doctor examined the body to discover which of the twenty-three stab wounds had caused Caesar to die.

- Odoacer, leader of a Germanic tribe, became the first non-Roman ruler of Italy. After many battles and a long siege with his rival Theodric, leader of the Ostrogoths, Theodric and Odoacer signed a peace treaty and had a feast to celebrate in AD 493. At the feast, Theodric stabbed Odoacer to death.

- Constantine Hangerli, Prince of Wallachia, was executed in 1799 by being strangled, shot twice in the chest, stabbed and then beheaded, too, for good measure. His head and other remains were put on display outside his palace.

- Roman emperor Nero made several attempts to kill his mother, Agrippina (who had poisoned her husband, the Emperor Claudius, with mushrooms). He tried several times with poison, he sabotaged her bedroom so that the ceiling collapsed on top of her bed and he arranged for her boat to be sunk in the Bay of Naples. None of them were successful until, in AD 59, Agrippina was clubbed to death by an assassin.

- Russian revolutionary Leon Trotsky spent the last years of his life in exile in Mexico. In 1940, he was killed by an assassin who attacked him with an ax. Trotsky put up a fight before his bodyguards came to his aid, taking a bite out of the assassin's leg, but he died at the hospital the following day.

- **Roman emperor Elagabalus was murdered by his own bodyguards in AD 222 and his body thrown in a sewer.**

- Spanish conquistador Pedro de Valdivia was killed in battle in 1553, defeated by indigenous South Americans. There are different gruesome stories about what happened to him: One says he was forced to drink molten gold because of his reputation as a greedy man (like the ancient Roman Crassus). Another says that his heart was ripped from his body and passed around for his victors to suck the blood while a drinking cup was made from his skull.

Life After Death

Dead bodies sometimes go on to have adventures of their own: standing trial, being crowned queen, traveling the world or even winning the Olympics.

- In 2006, a Democratic Party candidate won an election for a seat on the county board of Monroe, North Carolina, despite having been dead for a month. Election officials knew that the man had died, but they didn't tell the voters.

- Vietnamese president Ho Chi Minh died in 1969, and his embalmed body was put on display in the Ho Chi Minh Mausoleum in Hanoi, where it can still be visited. Ho Chi Minh had wanted to be cremated, however, which he thought was more hygienic and wouldn't take up valuable land that could be used for farming.

- **Oldest Dead Man**

  The man thought to be the oldest living resident of Itami, Japan, had in fact been dead for several years. The man's body was discovered lying on his bed in 2005, and might have been dead for as long as ten years. The man, who would have been 107 if he had been alive, had shared the house with his three sons, who were in their seventies. They rarely bothered their father, although one of them said he had wondered recently if there was something the matter with him.

Missing Mussolini

Benito Mussolini, the Italian dictator, was executed in 1945. Afterward, his body was hung upside down in a square in Milan before being buried in an unmarked grave. But the following year, Mussolini's body was dug up by some of his supporters and hidden. The location of the body was a mystery for several months until it was found in a small trunk just outside Milan. The body remained unburied for ten years while Italian authorities decided what to do with it. It was finally buried at Mussolini's birthplace.

- The Duke of Monmouth was beheaded as a traitor after he led a rebellion against James II of England. After he died, his family realized they didn't have a portrait of him, so his head was stuck back on to his body while he had his portrait painted.

- Like Russian revolutionary leader Lenin before him, Joseph Stalin's body was embalmed after his death in 1953. Stalin lay next to Lenin in Red Square in Moscow for eight years, until Stalin fell out of favor. His body was removed and buried underneath the Kremlin Wall.

EVITA'S TRAVELS

Eva Perón, the wife of the Argentinian president Juan Perón, was a popular political figure and greatly mourned when she died in 1952, aged just thirty-three. Her husband spent a large sum of money having her embalmed, a process that took about a year, and planned to place her in a grand tomb where she would be on display to the public, but in the meantime, the body was displayed in her former office.

However, the government was overthrown before the tomb was finished. Perón fled the country, and the location of Eva Perón's body was a mystery for sixteen years — in fact, it spent some time in an army general's flat and in a wooden crate in the attic of a military building, labeled "radio equipment." It was finally revealed that the embalmed body had been transported to Milan, Italy, and buried under a different name.

In 1972, Juan Perón returned to Argentina, to become president for a second time. He asked for his wife's body to be sent back to her homeland, too, but he died before it could be arranged. Eva Perón's body was displayed in Buenos Aires for two years, until the government was overthrown once again, and she was at last buried in a Buenos Aires cemetery.

- Saint Thomas Becket, Archbishop of Canterbury, was executed on the steps of Canterbury Cathedral on the orders of Henry II of England. Hundreds of years after Becket's death, King Henry VIII ordered Becket's bones to be dug up and put on trial. They were found guilty of treason and burned.

- ## Gruesome Coronation

  Inês de Castro was married to the future king of Portugal, Pedro I, but died before Pedro became king. Legend has it that Pedro had Inês's body dug up two years after her death, dressed the corpse in rich robes and crowned it Queen of Portugal. Pedro is supposed to have made all his courtiers swear allegiance to the dead woman and kiss her withered hand. The story might not be true, but Inês de Castro's body was definitely removed from her first grave and moved to a different tomb, where it remains, next to Pedro's tomb.

- Kintpuash, a Native American known as Captain Jack, was hanged in 1873 after the killing of an American general who had been sent to negotiate with him. A day after his body had been buried, it was dug up by grave robbers and embalmed. It then traveled around America as a fairground attraction. Kintpuash's head was sent to the Army Medical Museum in Washington, DC, and later to the Smithsonian Institute. The Smithsonian finally returned the head to his descendants in 1984.

- Dutch politician Gilles van Ledenberg was arrested for treason and killed himself in 1618. His trial continued despite his death and, the following year, his embalmed body was hanged from a gallows, still in its coffin. It stayed there for three weeks before it was buried, but an angry mob later dug up van Ledenberg's body and threw it in a ditch. Eventually, the body was reburied in a secret location.

Dead Men Walking

After the restoration of the monarchy in England in 1660, the bodies of Oliver Cromwell and two other men were dug up and executed for their involvement in the execution of the previous king, Charles I. John Bradshaw had been the judge at the trial of Charles I and died in 1659. Henry Ireton, who died in 1651, had signed Charles I's death warrant. Cromwell, Bradshaw and Ireton were dug up and displayed in chains for a day at Tyburn gallows in London, then at sunset, they were beheaded. The bodies were thrown into a pit, while the heads were stuck on pikes and displayed at Westminster Hall. Oliver Cromwell's head went on to have further adventures. (See page 23.)

- Kim Il-sung, President of North Korea, died in 1994. He was embalmed and placed in a glass coffin, which is still on display at Kumsusan Memorial Palace.

Paine's Remains

The English writer and philosopher Thomas Paine died in 1809 in America, where he had spent much of his life, and was buried in New York. William Cobbett, a campaigner and journalist in England, had been influenced by Paine and believed that his grave wasn't being respected in New York. In 1819, he set off to America to bring Paine's body back to his homeland, where he wanted the philosopher to be given a fitting memorial. Unfortunately, Paine had been an opponent of the monarchy in England, and so Cobbett's plans were refused. Paine's remains were stored in Cobbett's attic until his death in 1835.

After that, it's thought that Cobbett's son sold off the bones. At one time, an English bishop claimed to have part of Paine's skull and right arm on display on his mantelpiece, a man in France said he owned a rib and a woman in England claimed Paine's jawbone.

THE BANDIT WHO WOULDN'T GIVE UP

Elmer McCurdy robbed a bank in Oklahoma, U.S., in 1911. A gang of men chased after him, and McCurdy was killed in a shoot-out. No one came to claim McCurdy's body, so the undertaker had it embalmed and charged people to see "The Bandit Who Wouldn't Give Up." After several years, a man posing as McCurdy's relative claimed the body and put it on display in a touring sideshow. Eventually, McCurdy's body ended up in an amusement park in California, where everyone assumed it was a model. One day in 1976, a television drama was being filmed at the amusement park. When a crew member moved McCurdy's body and an arm fell off, it became clear that it wasn't a model after all. McCurdy was finally buried in a cemetery in Oklahoma in 1977.

- In 1478, Jacopo de'Pazzi plotted to assassinate the ruler of Florence and was hanged for his crime. His burial took place in the family vault on church grounds, which was followed by very bad weather. People thought that God was offended because a traitor had been buried in holy ground, and they threatened to riot. So monks dug up the body and buried it elsewhere. The story went that wailing sounds could be heard coming from the new grave. Finally, Jacopo de'Pazzi's body was dug up again by an angry mob, dragged through the streets of Florence and thrown into the River Arno.

- Ancient Greek king Leonidas I of Sparta was killed in battle against the Persians. The Persian king gave orders for Leonidas's dead body to be crucified and his head cut off and displayed on a stake.

- Visitors can see various mummified bodies at Saint Michan's church in Dublin, Ireland. Conditions there have preserved the bodies of, among others, a nun, a man believed to have been a crusader (whose body has been cut in half to fit into the coffin), various members of the 1798 Irish rebellion who were executed by the British and an unknown man missing a hand and both feet.

- Admiral Horatio Nelson was killed at the Battle of Trafalgar in 1805. His body was preserved in a barrel of brandy until his ship got back to England, where he was given a grand state funeral. Legend has it that sailors drank the alcohol using straws while Nelson's body was being transported.

- George Gordon, Earl of Huntly, was a Scottish rebel who opposed the rule of Mary, Queen of Scots. He was defeated in battle and captured, and he died soon afterward. In order for his lands to be confiscated, he had to be convicted of treason. So Huntly's body was preserved, sent to Edinburgh and put on trial in 1563. Not surprisingly, he didn't have much to say in his defence and was found guilty. Huntly's corpse was beheaded.

- Pope Formosus died in 896. The following year, under the orders of Pope Stephen VI, his body was dug up, dressed as a Pope and propped up on a throne to face charges against him. The corpse was found guilty. Three fingers were cut off his right hand so that he couldn't bless anybody in the afterlife, then the rest of the body was thrown into the River Tiber. Formosus's body was later fished out by a monk and reburied once Stephen VI had died.

- German knight, Christian Friedrich von Kahlbutz, died in 1702. In 1792, his coffin was opened in order to move the body to a cemetery, along with the other coffins in the family tomb where he was buried. Strangely, Kahlbutz's body had not decayed, although all of the other bodies had. His body doesn't seem to have been embalmed in any way. It is still on display in the village of Kampehl.

- More than five thousand years ago, a man was walking in the Alps when he was attacked, shot with an arrow and killed. The ice preserved him so well that when he was discovered by hikers in 1991, he still had hair, skin and some of his clothing. Known as Ötzi, he is now displayed at the South Tyrol Museum of Archaeology in Bolzano, Italy. But modern preservation techniques are not as good as the ice, and scientists are battling to preserve Ötzi.

BENTHAM'S MUMMY

As requested in his will, the philosopher Jeremy Bentham's body was dissected after his death, then the skeleton was reconstructed and dressed in Bentham's own clothes. The head was mummified, but the process didn't turn out very well, so a wax head was made and placed on top of the skeleton instead. Bentham's skeleton is displayed at University College, London, in a glass case, complete with its wax head. The mummified head used to lie on the floor of the case, but after it had been stolen various times, and was once held for ransom by students, it was removed and stored securely elsewhere.

← real head kept in safe

Livingstone's Last Journey

British explorer Dr. David Livingstone died in 1873 in a remote part of Zambia. His African friends, Susi and Chuma, were determined that Livingstone's body should make the difficult journey to the African coast, 1 500 km (930 mi.) away, and then by sea to his homeland. They carefully removed Livingstone's internal organs, burying them in the village, and preserved the body with salt and brandy, drying it out in the hot sun over fifteen days. The body was then bound in calico, put inside a bark coffin covered in sailcloth and carried to the coast — a journey that lasted nine months. Susi and Chuma alerted British authorities, and Livingstone's body was taken to England, where it was buried in Westminster Abbey.

- Chinese leader Mao Ze Dong died in 1976. His mummified body is displayed in a mausoleum in Tiananmen Square, Beijing.

- King Harold I of England died in 1040. When his half-brother Harthacanute became king later the same year, he had Harold's body dug up, beheaded and thrown into a swamp.

Immortal Elspeth

Scottish woman Elspeth Buchan was convinced that she was immortal. She announced to her group of Christian followers that, although she might appear to have died, she would actually have been taken straight up to heaven, and that she would return for her followers six months afterward, or, if their faith wasn't strong enough, ten years afterward, or fifty years afterward if that failed, too. She died in 1791. Six months later, nothing happened. Nothing happened ten years later, either, despite the hopes of her followers. After fifty years, there were still two of her followers left. When the anniversary of Buchan's death passed without anything happening, they gave up their faith.

KILLING VAMPIRES

In 1725, Peter Plogojowitz died and was buried in Kisilova, in modern-day Serbia. After his death, there was a spate of other deaths in the area, and locals became convinced that Plogojowitz must be a vampire who was feasting on them. He was dug up and the body examined for evidence of vampirism — various signs, such as blood around the corpse's mouth and lack of decomposition, made the villagers even more convinced that he was a vampire. They impaled the body on a stake, burned it and buried the ashes outside church grounds.

In 1892, Mercy Brown died of tuberculosis in Rhode Island, U.S. Her mother and sister had both died from the same disease. Soon after Mercy's death, her brother, also suffering from tuberculosis, became a lot worse. The rumor spread that a vampire was the cause of the deaths in the family, and Mercy's father took it so seriously that he dug up his daughter. Her body was well preserved, which was evidence enough for Mr. Brown. He took out her heart, burned it and gave the ashes, mixed with water, to his sick son. Despite the fact that the son also died, Mr. Brown seemed convinced that the vampire was dead.

- Qin Shi Huang, the first emperor of China, died on a tour of the country. Afraid that the emperor's death would cause a rebellion, the prime minister kept it a secret until they arrived home two months later. "Discussions" were held with the dead emperor's body every day throughout the journey. Carriages containing fish went before and after the emperor's carriage to disguise the smell of the body.

- In 1925, caving fan Floyd Collins was killed when he became trapped in a rockfall in a cave in Kentucky, U.S. His death became famous, and his family decided to capitalize on it: They had his body dug up, embalmed and put in a glass coffin. They installed it at the entrance to the cave where he died as a ghastly tourist attraction. It remained there until someone stole it, although the body was later returned minus the left leg, which was never recovered.

Dead Champion

Arrichion of Phigaleia was an ancient Greek Olympic champion in the sport of *pankration*, a type of violent wrestling in which people were sometimes seriously injured or killed. Arrichion was fighting in his third Olympic championship when his opponent leaped onto his back, strangling him from behind. Arrichion managed to force his opponent off his back, causing the other fighter to break his ankle. Arrichion died just at the moment his opponent signaled his own defeat. The judges conferred and announced Arrichion as the winner — a champion for the third time but a dead one.

- John Wycliffe was an English priest who had different ideas from those of the Catholic Church in the fourteenth century. Forty-five years after his death, the Church declared him a heretic, burned the books he had written and dug up and burned his body, casting the ashes into the River Swift.

• Mummies' Fates

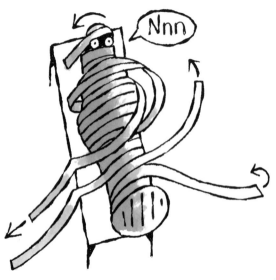

The most famous mummies in the world are Egyptian ones, preserved by taking out internal organs, drying and treating the body with salt, then wrapping it in bandages. Thousands of Egyptian mummies have been removed from their resting places, and many have suffered dreadful fates. In the nineteenth century, Egyptian mummies were mixed as a dye in a paint color called "mummy brown," dissected in front of audiences at events known as "unrollings" and even used as medicine. In 1907, thousands of mummies were burned as land was cleared for the Aswan Dam in Egypt.

• Catherine Wampmartin, a former nun who had married an Italian religious reformer, died in Oxford, England, in 1553. Four years later, her body was dug up, tried for heresy and thrown on a dung heap in the dean of Christ Church's stables.

• Nils Dacke was the leader of a Swedish peasant revolt. He died in 1543, trying to escape after a battle against the king of Sweden's troops. His dead body was executed, then chopped up, and various bits of him were sent to different parts of Sweden for public display.

WELL PRESERVED

Holy toe

Francis Xavier, later named a saint, was a Spanish missionary. He died in 1552 on a Chinese island, and his body was treated with quicklime to speed decomposition so that his bones could be returned to Spain. When the body was dug up after several weeks, it hadn't decomposed at all. It was sent to the Basilica of Bom Jesus in Goa, India, where it remains today in a glass box. Over the centuries, various bits of Saint Francis have gone missing. In 1554, he lost one of his toes to a visitor who wanted a souvenir, and three more toes disappeared in the same way. In 1614, the right arm was removed below the elbow — this was the arm Saint Francis used to give his blessing, and it was wanted by a church in Rome. Many other Catholic saints' bodies are said to be miraculously preserved, although tests on some of them have shown that they were in fact embalmed — over the centuries, the records had become lost.

SELF-MUMMIFYING MONKS

Shingon Buddhist monks in Japan actually made themselves into mummies using a special diet and meditation. The last known self-mummified monk died in 1877, and since then, the practice has been illegal. The monks achieved their grisly aim over a period of several years. They began by spending one thousand days eating only nuts and seeds, while doing lots of physical work, in an effort to reduce body fat as much as possible. The next one thousand days were spent eating only the bark and roots of a particular pine tree, making the monks extremely thin and dehydrated. Then, during the last part of this period, the monks could only drink a special tea made from urushi tree sap. The sap is poisonous, and it caused the monks to dehydrate further still, and it had the added effect of killing off the various bugs that aid decomposition of a human body. Then, in the final one thousand days (or perhaps fewer), the monks sat alone in stone rooms, meditating. Every morning, the monks would ring a bell, and on the morning no bell could be heard, the room was sealed up. Later, the monks would be placed in a shrine. The last monk to mummify himself, Tetsuryou-kai, can be seen today at the Nangakuji temple in Japan, and there are various other monks on display in other temples.

Glittering Composer

Ludwig van Beethoven died in 1827. One hundred and eighty years later, some of his remains were made into three diamonds. The company Lifegem, which specializes in turning cremated human bodies into diamonds, made the precious stones using a few strands of the composer's hair from a collection of famous hair stored in Connecticut, U.S. Two commercial companies offer to turn a cremated dead body into a diamond by extracting carbon and heating it to extremely high temperatures. An average body contains enough carbon to make more than fifty diamonds.

- Li Lin Fu, an important official in the Chinese Tang dynasty, died in AD 753. The Chinese emperor awarded him a grand funeral but, before it could take place, Li Lin Fu's rival accused the dead man of being involved in a rebellion. Li Lin Fu was found guilty. The coffin was opened and symbols of Li Lin Fu's honor were removed from the body, which was then given a commoner's burial. All his descendants were exiled.

The Real Jesse James

American outlaw Jesse James had carried out various bank robberies before he was shot and killed in 1882. His body was buried in his family's garden, then moved to a cemetery some years later. Meanwhile, a man called Frank Dalton claimed to be the real Jesse James, having staged his own death so that he could live the rest of his life unrecognized. When Dalton died in 1951, the sheriff who examined his body was convinced that the man was actually Jesse James. Many years later, in 1995, Jesse James was dug up, and tests proved the remains to be of the real Jesse James. Dalton's remains were also dug up and tested, but ironically they were found to belong to someone else entirely: The biggest clue was that the body in Dalton's grave only had one arm, while Dalton had had two.

• Stuffed Emperor

Roman emperor Valerian was defeated and captured by his enemy, Persian king Shapur I in AD 260. He spent the rest of his life imprisoned by Shapur, who humiliated Valerian by leading him around in chains or using him as a stool when Shapur was mounting his horse.

Eventually, Shapur had Valerian killed; according to one story, Valerian offered Shapur a large ransom for his release, and Shapur responded by forcing him to drink molten gold. After Valerian's death, Shapur had him skinned and stuffed with straw, and put him on display in a temple.

• A community of Capuchin monks who lived in Palermo, Sicily, buried their dead in a grotto behind their church. When it became full and the bodies were about to be moved somewhere else, it was discovered that many of the bodies had been amazingly well preserved, the result of natural conditions in the limestone grotto. The people of Palermo decided that they wanted to be preserved in the same way, and burial in the grotto became a special privilege of the most important and wealthy people of Palermo. The bodies were embalmed as well as being placed in the grotto, which was extended to form the Catacombs of the Capuchins. More than eight thousand bodies are buried there, some better preserved than others. The last one was placed there in 1920. Today, the Catacombs of the Capuchins are open to visitors.

• A Mexican woman called Julia Pastrana was exhibited as "The Bearded and Hairy Lady" due to the long, straight hair growing on her face and body. When she died in 1860 her "manager," Theodore Lent, had her body embalmed and continued to exhibit her. Julia Pastrana's body was still on display as late as the 1970s in Norway. It was stolen in 1979 but eventually found and is now stored in the Oslo Forensic Institute, at last away from prying eyes.

Fatal Mistakes

It could happen to anyone ... making a bungee jump with a rope that's too long, hurling yourself at an "unbreakable" window or simply forgetting your parachute.

- ## Boiled Baker

    The Reverend Baker traveled to the Pacific islands in the 1860s, on a mission to convert the people who lived there to Christianity. He was visiting a remote Fijian village when he made the fatal mistake of touching the chief's head. Unfortunately, this was strictly forbidden, and the villagers clubbed Baker to death, along with the rest of his group, and then cooked and ate them. In 2003, the people of the Fijian village made an official apology to the descendants of Reverend Baker by inviting them to the village and giving them hospitality and gifts.

- In 1993, a Canadian lawyer was demonstrating that the windows in his twenty-fourth story office were unbreakable. One of them gave way, and he fell to his death.

- In 1987, an experienced parachutist in North Carolina prepared to make a video of a skydiving lesson. He attached the camera to his helmet, while the recording device and power supply were strapped to his back. He jumped from the plane, filming the instructor and his student, then realized he had forgotten to put on his own parachute.

- Johann Underwald, a Swiss mathematician, made a fatal error in his calculations in 1999. He made a 75 m (250 ft.) bungee jump with a rope measuring 100 m (330 ft.).

- **Metal Dectector**

  Only a few months after he became U.S. president in 1881, James Garfield was shot by an assassin. Doctors struggled to find a bullet lodged somewhere in the president's body but could not find it. The inventor Alexander Graham Bell devised a metal detector to try and find the bullet, and Garfield was cut open in several different places. Bell later realized that the metal detector couldn't tell the difference between a bullet and the metal springs of the bed. Garfield died of blood poisoning.

Ironic Fates

The king who bled to death as a result of his own victory cannon, the philosopher who leaped to his death trying to prove he was immortal and the conqueror who died of a nosebleed ...

- James II of Scotland defeated the English at Roxburgh Castle. After the victory, a cannon was fired in celebration, but it exploded. A piece of wood sent flying by the explosion chopped off James's leg, and he bled to death.

- A Polish man was so afraid of being burgled that he set up booby traps around his house. His garage was fitted with guns, which killed him in 1996 while he was opening the doors.

- Pillaging conqueror Attila the Hun died of a nosebleed. It was his wedding night, and he had had a lot to drink.

- A Vietnamese man became famous and appeared on TV because of his seemingly amazing ability to withstand electric shocks. He died in 2006 when he tried to repair an electric generator without turning off the power.

- In 1985, a group of lifeguards in New Orleans had a party to celebrate a year without anyone drowning in their area. After the party, a guest at the party, not a lifeguard himself, was found drowned in the deep end of the swimming pool.

- According to one report, the ancient Greek philosopher Empedocles died when he threw himself into an active volcano, Mount Etna in Sicily, supposedly to prove that he was immortal.

Yes, I'm immortal.

Uh, maybe not. Urk.

- In 1911, Bobby Leach rode in a barrel over Niagara Falls. He broke most of the bones in his body but, unlike many other people who tried the stunt, he survived. After his recovery, he made a living by touring the world, telling the tale of his adventure, until he slipped on some fruit peel, and died of the injuries.

- A Christian preacher called Franck Kabele in Gabon, West Africa, claimed that he could walk on water as Jesus had. In 2006, he led his congregation to the beach, telling them that he was about to walk across the Komo estuary. He strode out into the water and was soon submerged. He was never seen again.

- Franz Reichell, known as "the flying tailor," was killed in 1912 demonstrating the coat-parachute he had invented. He jumped from a height of 60 m (200 ft.) from the Eiffel Tower wearing the parachute, although he'd told everyone he would use a dummy for the demonstration.

- **American William Bullock was also killed by his own invention. In 1867, he was tinkering with the web rotary press, a successful new printing press, when his leg became caught in the machine and was crushed. Gangrene set in, and Bullock died during the operation to amputate his leg.**

- In 892, Sigurd I of Orkney killed his enemy Máel Brigte of Moray in battle. He fixed Máel Brigte's head to his saddle in triumph, but the teeth of the severed head pierced Sigurd's skin, causing a wound that became septic and killed him.

- Jerome Rodale, American writer, publisher and longevity expert, appeared on a television talk show in 1971 aged seventy-two, claiming that he would live to one hundred and stating that he had "never felt better." During the show, while a fellow guest was being interviewed, he had a heart attack and died.

- Austrian composer Arnold Schoenberg was afraid of the number thirteen. All his life, he was especially terrified of Friday the thirteenth and any multiples of thirteen. He dreaded his sixty-fifth birthday in 1939 because both sixty-five and thirty-nine are multiples of thirteen. In 1950, on his seventy-sixth birthday, an astrologer wrote to Schoenberg warning him that the year was ill-fated because seven plus six equal thirteen, something that hadn't occurred to Schoenberg. He became frightened and depressed and finally died on Friday the thirteenth July 1951, while he was still seventy-six years old.

- Deacon William Brodie was a wealthy Scottish carpenter who turned to burglary when he became short of money. He was tried and sentenced to be hanged. His woodworking skills were put to use when he designed and made the gallows on which he was hanged in 1788.

- Inventor Thomas Midgley devised a system of ropes and pulleys to get him in and out of bed: He became entangled in the ropes and was strangled in 1944.

- Clement Vallandigham, U.S. Congressman and lawyer, died while he was representing the defendant in a murder trial. He explained to his colleagues how the alleged murder victim could have shot himself while drawing his gun, rather than being shot by Vallandigham's client. Then he demonstrated drawing a gun while standing up from a kneeling position. The gun, which Vallandigham had thought was unloaded, went off, and he died a few days later. His client in the court case was acquitted.

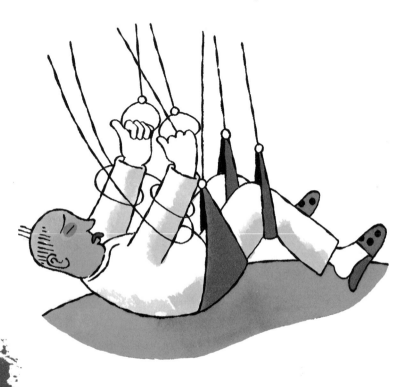

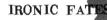

- Three men were looking for scrap metal in Vietnam in 2006 when they discovered an unexploded bomb. They decided it was a good idea to roll it down a hill — it wasn't, and the bomb exploded, killing all three of them.

- A man in Hawaii decided to climb several meters (feet) up a koa tree, a valuable hardwood, and saw off a branch. Unfortunately, he sawed off the branch directly above him, which bashed him on the head and killed him.

- In 1999, an impatient Ukrainian fisherman decided to connect a cable to his home power supply and trail the other end into the River Tereblya in order to electrocute some fish. Dead fish floated to the surface, and the man entered the water to get them, forgetting to remove the live cable.

- A Serbian man was killed by his own bomb in 2008. He was on the run from the police, wanted for murder and robbery, and his friend had lent him several thousand euros to help him escape. He didn't want to pay back the money. He decided it would be a good idea to plant a homemade bomb underneath his friend's car. It exploded as he was trying to attach it.

- In 2008, a Bulgarian biology teacher had been conducting some chemistry experiments and had various bottles full of chemicals in her car. Perhaps because of the smell of the chemicals, she decided to stop the car and pour them down a drain. Whatever the chemicals were, they reacted extremely violently, blowing off a manhole cover and killing her instantly.

- Two Italian brothers-in-law were having an argument about which of them should have the last place in the family tomb. Finally, one of them stabbed the other, killing his brother-in-law and settling the matter, not in his own favor.

- French mountaineer Gerard Hommel had climbed Mount Everest six times. He died in 1993 when he fell off a stepladder trying to change a lightbulb.

- In 1837, Englishman Robert Cocking became the first person to die in a parachute accident when the parachute he had designed failed to open.

- In 1994, an American man grabbed a hot dog from a convenience store, stuffed it into his mouth and left without paying. Police found him later, not far from the store, having choked to death on the hot dog.

Last Words
and Epitaphs

The last thing people ever
say might be witty, grim,
optimistic or unexpected.
People have less control
over what's carved on
their gravestones ...

- One man was concerned that visitors to his graveside in Massachusetts should know about his accomplishments:

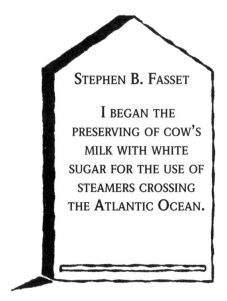

STEPHEN B. FASSET

I BEGAN THE PRESERVING OF COW'S MILK WITH WHITE SUGAR FOR THE USE OF STEAMERS CROSSING THE ATLANTIC OCEAN.

- The composer Chopin was dying of tuberculosis but feared an even more dreadful fate — his last words were:

Swear to make them cut me open so that I won't be buried alive.

- Ivanka Perko had lived through Nazi occupation and made a daring escape from her native Slovenia (then part of Yugoslavia) to settle in Australia. At the age of seventy-three, she had developed a condition that made her skin extremely delicate. She dropped a banana on her leg and died from complications due to the wound. Her last words were:

I can't believe, after all this time, it was a bloody banana that killed me.

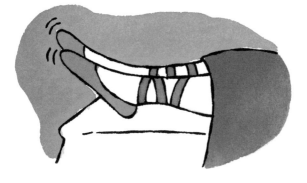

- Anna Pavlova was a ballerina most famous for her "Dying Swan" dance. When she died in 1931, her last words were, "Get my swan costume ready."

- Elizabeth Picket died in 1781 "in consequence of her clothes taking fire," and her headstone carries some safety advice:

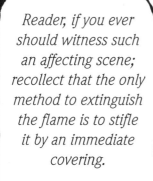

Reader, if you ever should witness such an affecting scene; recollect that the only method to extinguish the flame is to stifle it by an immediate covering.

- British prime minister Henry John Temple's last words were:

Die, my dear doctor? That's the last thing I shall do!

And it was.

- The philosopher Karl Marx didn't think much of last words. His were:

Go on, get out! Last words are for fools who haven't said enough!

- In the Shetland Islands lies Donald Robertson, whose gravestone tells a story:

A peaceable, quiet man, and to all appearances a sincere Christian ... his death was caused by the stupidity of Laurence Tulloch, who sold him nitre instead of Epsom salts, by which he was killed in the space of five hours after taking a dose of it.

- These were the last words of the inventor Thomas Edison:

It's very beautiful over there.

No one knows whether he was talking about the view from his window or a vision of the afterlife.

- Paul Claudel, a French writer, is reported to have said some rather unglamorous last words:

Doctor, do you think it could have been the sausage?

- Ramón Maria Narváez y Campos, First Duke of Valencia, was asked by a priest if he forgave his enemies while on his deathbed in 1868. He replied:

  I do not have to forgive my enemies. I have had them all shot.

- Actor Lou Costello had some cheerful last words:

  That was the best ice cream soda I ever tasted.

- Slipping on a banana peel and dying is a dreadful fate that someone decided to immortalize on Anna Hopewell's headstone in Vermont:

  HERE LIES THE BODY
  OF OUR ANNA
  DONE TO DEATH BY
  A BANANA
  IT WASN'T THE FRUIT THAT
  LAID HER LOW
  BUT THE SKIN OF THE THING
  THAT MADE HER GO.

- Margaret Bent's relatives retained a sense of humor about her death. The epitaph on her tombstone in Dorset, England, reads:

**HERE LIES THE BODY
OF MARGARET BENT
SHE KICKED UP HER HEELS
AND AWAY SHE WENT**

- The American actor John Barrymore died in 1942 after uttering these words:

Die? I should say not, dear fellow. No Barrymore would allow such a conventional thing to happen to him.

- Ellen Shannon's grave in Pennsylvania tells a sad story:

*Who was fatally burned
March 21, 1870
by the explosion of
a lamp filled with
"R.E. Danforth's
Non-Explosive
Burning Fluid"*

- The French grammarian Dominique Bouhours was true to his profession right until the end. His last words were, *"Je vais ou je vas mourir, l'un et l'autre se dit ou se dissent,"* which can be translated as:

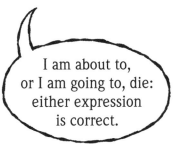

I am about to, or I am going to, die: either expression is correct.

- British member of parliament Lady Nancy Astor, MP, was surrounded by members of her family on her deathbed. Her last words were:

Am I dying, or is this my birthday?

- This inscription is from a tombstone in Nova Scotia, Canada:

HERE LIES
EZEKIAL
AIKLE
AGE 102

*The Good
Die Young*

- The Norwegian playwright Henrik Ibsen's last words were:

On the contrary!

He was responding to a nurse's comment to a visitor that he was getting a bit better.

- The epitaph on William Shakespeare's tombstone carries a warning:

> *GOOD FREND*
> *FOR JESUS SAKE*
> *FORBEARE*
> *TO DIG THE DUST*
> *ENCLOASED HEARE.*
> *BLEST BE YE MAN*
> *YT SPARES THES*
> *STONES*
> *AND CURST BE HE*
> *YT MOVES MY BONES.*

- John Sedgwick, a Union general in the American Civil War, was shot and killed by a Confederate sniper just after he'd uttered these words:

They couldn't hit an elephant at this distance.

- Pope Alexander VI died in 1503 at the age of seventy-two, having been taken ill with a fever. His last words were:

Wait a minute ...

- No one knows who is buried under this tombstone in Vermont:

I WAS
SOMEBODY.

WHO, IS
NO BUSINESS
OF YOURS.

Index

Are You Afraid Yet?
The Science Behind Scary Stuff

Written by Stephen James O'Meara,
illustrated by Jeremy Kaposy

Whether you're a skeptic or a believer, this illustrated investigation into the stuff that scares us — and the gruesome science behind it — will make your skin crawl and your spine tingle. Don't miss severed heads that blink, real-life werewolves and more.

Hardcover 978-1-55453-294-0
Paperback 978-1-55453-295-7

100% Pure Fake
Gross Out Your Friends and Family with 25 Great Special Effects!

Written by Lyn Thomas

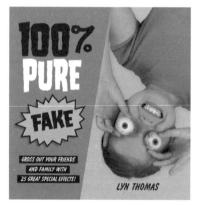

Parents, beware! This book has perfected the art of scaring the pants off unsuspecting friends and family. Pranksters will delight in the 25 kid-tested projects that are sure to amaze, alarm and totally disgust everyone around them.

Hardcover 978-1-55453-290-2